FUND A FIELD
CHARITIES STARTED BY KIDS!
BY MELISSA SHERMAN PEARL AND DAVID A. SHERMAN

Published in the United States of America by Cherry Lake Publishing
Ann Arbor, Michigan
www.cherrylakepublishing.com

Reading Adviser: Marla Conn MS, Ed., Literacy specialist, Read-Ability, Inc.

Photo Credits: Photos used with permission from FundaField, Cover, 1, 5, 9, 11, 15, 17, 19, 21; © Csaba Peterdi / Shutterstock.com, 7; © lkpro / Shutterstock.com, 13

LIBRARY OF CONGRESS CATALOGING-IN-PUBLICATION DATA HAS BEEN FILED AND IS AVAILABLE AT CATALOG.LOC.GOV

Cherry Lake Publishing would like to acknowledge the
work of The Partnership for 21st Century Learning. Please
visit *www.p21.org* for more information.

Printed in the United States of America
Corporate Graphics

FUNDAFIELD

CONTENTS

HOW DO THEY HELP?

WORLD CUP INSPIRES A WORLD MISSION

Many kids in Africa deal with political unrest, **malnutrition**, and disease. For some, even going to school can be a challenge. FUNDaFIELD has found a way to make kids happier and help them have some fun, too.

In 2006, Kyle and Garrett Weiss went with their family to the FIFA World Cup in Germany. During the

More than 1 billion people around the world watched the 2014 FIFA World Cup final.

THINK!

The Weiss family has made it a tradition to go to World Cup matches all over the world. Is there any kind of event you'd want to travel the world to see? Where would you want to go?

5

match between Iran and Angola, they noticed something amazing: the excitement of the Angolan fans!

After the match, Kyle and Garrett played soccer in the fields outside of the stadium with the Angolan fans. Because Angola had been in a civil war for so long, this was the country's very first World Cup game.

The brothers discovered that soccer was one of the biggest sources of joy in the country.

FIFA recognizes 211 national teams. Thirty-two teams play in the World Cup.

THINK!

What is your favorite sport? What things do you need to play it? Think about other kids who play the sport around the world. What might you be able to do to help them play?

When they returned to California, they got together with their buddies and talked about helping the young soccer fans in Africa. These soccer **enthusiasts** were super excited. They wanted to think big. Why not build a field where people can play? They'd raise money, get some land, and build a field. This was how FUNDaFIELD began.

Kyle was 13 years old and Garrett was 15 years old when they started FUNDaFIELD.

Soccer is the most popular sport in the world, with more than 3.5 billion fans worldwide. Do you know what people in most of the world call soccer? They call it "football," even though it is different from the sport of football that is played in the United States.

9

DIVIDE AND CONQUER

The boys **estimated** that building a field would cost $20,000. They started with car washes and bake sales. Then it hit them: a soccer field is a really big rectangle. They created an image of a soccer field and divided it into 20,000 squares. Who wouldn't want to buy a square for $1 to be a part of helping kids in Africa play soccer?

Kyle and Garrett's little sister, Kira, helped sell squares to raise money for the field.

How often is the FIFA World Cup held? If you guessed that the World Cup happens every four years, like the Olympics, you're right!

11

Raising the money was one thing. Building the field was a completely different story. They reached out to a number of organizations for help, but very few responded to the kids. One man told them that building in Angola wasn't very safe, but that he'd just finished building two new schools in South Africa and that people there were soccer-crazy. A partnership was born: He would build the field in South Africa that FUNDaFIELD would pay for.

It took two years for FUNDaFIELD to go from idea to completion of the first field.

LOOK!

In the South African FUNDaFIELD tournaments, the winning team earned a goat. Look online or at the library to find out what kinds of traditions might be honored in other countries.

13

The FUNDaFIELD team members made their first trip to South Africa in 2008 to see the field. They arrived with mounds of gear. They also held what became the first of many FUNDaFIELD tournaments.

By 2012, the FUNDaFIELD team had everything under control. The brothers had already visited Africa more than 15 times, so they truly understood the local communities. Their team and **contractors** did, too.

Playing sports with neighbors and friends helps create ties in your community.

LOOK!

Goats are important
to life in South
Africa. Look online
or at the library to
discover what benefits
goats add to the
communities there.

One team member noticed that schools located near the fields were getting busier. More kids signed up for school and were attending classes as often as possible when they knew they could play soccer nearby.

The Weiss brothers decided they should build future fields at schools. It was also important to them to focus on areas that had been affected by war or natural disasters. They believe sports are a great way to help people grow strong, thrive, and recover.

Building fields could help the kids become more successful in their futures.

ASK QUESTIONS!

Have you ever donated anything and seen it used later? How did it make you feel? Ask your friends and family if they have ever experienced that.

MAKING GOALS AND ACHIEVING GOALS

By the end of 2016, FUNDaFIELD had created soccer communities in Haiti, Kenya, South Africa, and Uganda. It had built 11 fields and held 15 tournaments that had hosted nearly 3,500 kids. It had also given away 13,000 pieces of gear such as jerseys, shorts, balls, socks, and cleats.

Kira Weiss also manages a project with FUNDaFIELD called Paper Beads From Africa that helps empower women in Uganda.

When people have a common interest, working hard to make something happen is easy. Do you and your friends have anything that you all love doing that could help people? Talk to them and see what you can do together.

Jobs and school have made it harder to run FUNDaFIELD, but the Weiss **siblings** remain involved, thanks to their reliable staff. Perhaps just as important as their cause is they learned that together, with one common goal, anyone can do anything.

The FUNDaFIELD motto is, "Because every kid deserves the chance to play."

There are lots of kids locally who cannot afford sports equipment. Create a fund-raiser for them. Place a box in your classroom and collect gently used equipment from your classmates. Then find a local organization where you can donate the goods.

GLOSSARY

contractors (KAHN-trakt-urz) people or companies that agree under contract to provide materials or labor for a service or job

enthusiasts (en-THOO-zee-ists) people who are highly interested in a particular activity or subject

estimated (ES-tuh-mate-id) formed an opinion or calculated the approximate amount, size, worth, or weight of something

malnutrition (mal-noo-TRISH-uhn) lack of proper food or nutrition

siblings (SIB-lingz) brothers or sisters

FIND OUT MORE

WEB SITES

www.fifa.com
Explore the Web site of the international soccer organization FIFA and see how it works to accomplish its goal of developing soccer everywhere.

www.fundafield.org
Learn more about FUNDaFIELD and what it does.

www.paperbeadsfromafrica.com
Find out more about the paper jewelry and accessories handcrafted by Ugandan women.

https://ussoccerfoundation.org/programs/passback
Read more about Passback, an organization that takes donations of soccer equipment and distributes them to children in underserved communities.

INDEX

24

ABOUT THE AUTHORS

David Sherman and Melissa Sherman Pearl are cousins who understand and appreciate that you don't have to be an adult to make a difference.